The Ride Home

STRATEGIES TO SUCCEED FOR
PARENTS AND COACHES

Jon Barth

Rise Above Leadership

Jon Barth/Rise Above Leadership
PO Box 122
Auburn, IL 62615
www.riseaboveleadership.com

Book Layout ©2017 BookDesignTemplates.com

Ordering Information:
Quantity sales. Special discounts are available on quantity purchases by corporations, associations, and others. For details, contact the "Special Sales Department" at the address above.

The Ride Home: Strategies to Succeed for Parents and Coaches/Jon Barth. —1st ed.
ISBN 978-0-9993927-0-6 (paperback)

Contents

Dedicated to my wife, Sarah, and our children, Nathan, Jacob, and Hannah who inspire me to pursue my dreams and live my legacy every day!

This, I believe, is the purpose of sports.
To create better human beings.
When you develop champions you develop
people who will change the world.

—Jon Gordon

Foreword

My first three years of high school, the New Berlin High School basketball program had not come anywhere near a winning season. The people of this small, rural town near Springfield, Illinois stood behind their accomplished football team and their high caliber baseball team. However, the pride of the town seemed to fade away with the warm weather once basketball season came around. Several years of a second-rate team had eventually turned the eyes of the community, faculty, parents, and athletes to the coach of this inept team: Jon Barth.

Coach Barth had set numerous school records in his years playing basketball for New Berlin, and when he was given the opportunity to take over the coaching role of his hometown team, it was a dream come true for both himself and his New Berlin-based family. However, his talents on the court did not seem to translate over to coaching. That is if you measure coaching ability by wins and losses. However, as a player for Coach Barth, I had the opportunity to experience his coaching first-hand. In high school, I was a three-sport athlete with many years of experience.

And to this day, I can honestly say that Jon Barth has taught me more about life and about myself than any other coach in my athletic career.

You might be asking yourself why I praise the coach of my losing team. Well, the answer is simple: Coach Barth had the courage and audacity to teach character and leadership, not just basketball. His coaching style emphasized the idea that winning is not what is most important. He taught how sports are merely a way of developing oneself and preparing for life in the future. Unfortunately, few players and members of the community were willing to buy into this system.

After another losing season, more and more upset parents and athletes voiced their opinion: they did not want a coach who taught character, they wanted a coach who won basketball games. Coach Barth knew this but refused to overlook his morals and values. He stuck to his guns and continued to teach high school students about how to be successful at life through the medium of basketball. However, those who are excellent leaders of character are not always the best athletes, and the New Berlin community wanted athletes. Following my junior year, the school board made the decision to discontinue Coach Barth's contract as head coach. He would no longer be the New Berlin basketball coach, and after experiencing such a lack of support from his hometown, he would move away.

I, however, have nothing but admiration for Coach Barth. Those that scorned him as a coach did not understand the true impact that he had on his players. I vividly remember sitting in the locker room following one game. There was dead silence among the team as a feeling of disappointment swept through the room. Sweat dripped off our faces onto the floor of the hot, muggy room as if to cover up the tears of many. I am sure Coach Barth wanted to win that game, but he did not take out his frustration or anger on the team like many coaches would. He came into the locker room and told each and every player how proud he was of our effort and attitude throughout the season. I had never felt so motivated by a coach following a loss, and if that isn't coaching then I don't know what is.

As Coach Barth taught me, effort and attitude are the two things that I am always in control of. Life is 10% what happens to you and 90% how you respond to it, and Coach Barth lived what he taught. When met with challenges and adversity, he could have easily just abandoned his passion for teaching character and leadership. But instead, he clung to his morals and values. I am proud to have played under an excellent leader who is true to others as well as himself.

Jack Eason
U.S. Military Academy at West Point, Class of 2021

Introduction

Do sports teach character?

By simply participating in a sport, will a person automatically learn life lessons and increase character skills like discipline, cooperation, and loyalty? Participation in sports can, and very well should teach character. But without the proper perspective and guidance from mentors, the sports experience for many boys and girls can do more harm than good.

For many kids, the ride home with their parents or the post-game talk in the locker room with their coach are memories they would like to eliminate.

The good news is there is a simple solution, and all it requires is the proper perspective.

Providing a positive, life-changing sports experience for a child should be the objective of the most influential adults in this arena: their parents and their coaches. At the college level and beyond, the coach holds the primary influence over the person participating in sport, along with other adult mentors that the man or woman may seek. However, at the youth level (high school and earlier), the child is heavily influenced by their parents as well as their coach.

The relationship between parents and coaches of a child playing sports should be considered a partnership. By working together with the proper perspective, adults will not only provide an excellent experience for the child but create a foundation to help the child soar to their greatest potential as well.

In other words, let's use the sports experience to intentionally build character and teach life lessons so that players, parents, and coaches can all enjoy the journey!

The Ride Home was written to provide strategies and wisdom that may help parents and coaches look at things from a different perspective. We are all seeking the truth and we must be willing to empty our cup in the search for that truth. This journey is necessary if we truly want to reach our potential and experience our best, most authentic self.

Fear, incentive, and love are the primary motivating factors for most people. It is certainly possible to get results by using fear and incentive, but the question is what results are we looking for and at what cost are we willing to achieve those results? Motivation produced from love is more powerful and will last longer than both fear and incentive. Love will also produce results that should be the most valuable to us.

Do winning and other forms of achievement by themselves help our children become the best people they can be? The value of winning lies in the character put into the pursuit of excellence. Who we become in the process and the character we manifest is more important than any external result we can achieve. Winning without honor and integrity is a hollow victory.

Changing our perspective may help our child or team achieve better results than before. However, if the external results represent our motivation, our impact will be inconsistent and short-lived. Changing our perspective should occur out of our desire to put people, and the relationships with our children or players, first. We can live our legacy by being parents and coaches who strive for impact by relentlessly pursuing relationships.

I have participated in multiple sports my entire life, played NCAA Division II basketball in college, and coached from the college to youth levels. I have also been a part of the competitive experience from the parent side with our children who are currently ages 12, 10, and 5. I have found that external results may come and go, but our perspective determines whether or not we are using our competitive experience to be the type of people we truly want to be.

As a parent or coach, changing our perspective can revolutionize our competitive experience from one of frustration to one of joy. Changing our perspective can help us stop chasing results and start cultivating relationships. Changing our perspective can help us stop riding an emotional roller coaster with our competitive experience and help us start taking control to live our legacy.

Do we want to have a conversation with our child when they are 30 years old and realize they hated the car ride home?

Do we want to retire from coaching and forget the scores of the games and wish we had done more to help develop our players as people?

Do we want to enjoy the journey knowing we did our best and let the results take care of themselves?

We need to have conversations with our children and players to help guide them so they can use their competitive experience to be the best people they are capable of becoming.

We should not wait until we are on our deathbed to realize we are living our legacy every single day!

The Ride Home shares strategies for both parents and coaches so each side of this partnership can broaden their perspective and look at things from each point of view. Parents can benefit by realizing that a coach is responsible for not just one player, but all players on his or her team. Coaches can benefit by understanding that each child, while they may be part of a team, is an individual who should be mentored to bring out their unique greatness. According to John Wooden, "A coach, teacher, and leader...are all basic variations of being a parent."[1] Our children deserve a partnership that helps them win the game of life.

The time after a game is maybe the most impressionable time for a child playing sports and the most crucial for teaching life lessons. Coaches can create an environment for character-building with their post-game talk in the locker room and parents can enhance that with the conversation they have with their child on the way home. As children grow older, this conversation may not happen in the car, but instead at the kitchen table or in the living room in front of the television. If our children are not in the car with us after the game, as parents, we can use that time to reflect on the lessons we can discuss with them at the next opportunity. As coaches, we can use the ride home to reflect on how we are going to help the young people we work with move forward in a positive manner. No matter the context, these opportunities for guidance will be dictated by our perspective.

So on the ride home, let's take the road less traveled. It will make all the difference!

CHAPTER 1

Play for the Love of the Game

As a player, parent, or coach we have probably felt both the exhilaration of victory and the agony of defeat in a sports environment. But there is a better way that will allow us to experience the joy of the journey. Playing for the love of the game can guarantee a positive outcome every time we, and those we are leading, step into the arena of our competitive experience.

Several years ago, one of my close friends died in an automobile accident. Damien and I had grown up together going to school and playing sports and had both moved back to our hometown. We each had three children and they were all about the same ages. Damien coached my son's youth baseball team, and he was great at teaching the kids the fundamentals while also making sure they had fun.

After the first game of the season, Damien sent me a text message since I was at my other son's baseball game. He let me know that my son had done well. He also commented the kids "had a smile on their face and you could tell they were having fun," even though they lost on the scoreboard by quite a few runs.

I responded to him, "You are doing a good job with them and it will pay off in the future."

Damien responded with some great perspective. He said, "Wins and losses don't matter. If they are having fun and improving as the year goes on is the only thing that matters. It is nice to see several in that young group just really love playing the game. That is the nice thing. They want to play."

The world would be a better place if all youth sports coaches had Damien's perspective.

Winning is a Mindset

My favorite memory of Damien is one for which I was not actually present, but because I knew him so well I can picture the moment vividly in my mind. My wife relayed the story about what happened at the end of one of the baseball games he coached the summer he died. My son and his son, who were six years old at the time, went up and asked Damien if our team had won the game (we had lost the game by about ten runs, but we often did not tell the kids the score).

He asked the boys, "Do you think you won?"

They responded with huge smiles, "Yes!"

Damien proclaimed, "Well then you won the game." Then they celebrated like they had won the World Series.

Damien understood that if we give our best effort and have fun and enjoy playing the game the right way, then we are winners. Les Brown once declared that in this world there are winners, there are losers, and there are people who have not discovered how to win.[1] Sure, as we get older we start paying attention to the score, and things become more "competitive" than when we first begin. It is important to teach our children that they may not always win on the scoreboard but why should the measurement of how we feel about ourselves change?

Did we give our best effort? It shouldn't even be, "Did we play well?" Mistakes happen, slumps occur, and we can give our best effort but not necessarily play well. Our best effort at the moment does not always equate to our best performance.

Did we respect the game and play it the right way, no matter what the outcome? It is easy to feel good when things are going well, and just as easy to feel bad when things are not.

Did we learn something from our experience? In every game, win or lose, there are opportunities to learn how to improve our skills and how to improve our character as well.

The outcome does not determine the value of the process. As Coach Norman Dale declared in the famous movie *Hoosiers*, "If you put your effort and concentration into playing to your potential, to be the best that you can be, I don't care what the scoreboard says at the end of the game, in my book we're going to be winners!"[2] Winning is a mindset; it is a mindset that we have the character necessary for greatness already inside us. We just have to learn to focus on not letting things outside our control get in the way. It has nothing to do with the result and everything to do with the process.

Does this mean everyone deserves a trophy? Absolutely not! Giving an external reward for merely showing up is not teaching our children a life lesson. But if all we are playing for is the trophy so it can boost our ego, then that can be as detrimental as the participation trophy. What we need to do is inspire kids to play for the love of the game and help them internalize the results by using their experience to become a better person.

If it is not about winning then why do we even keep score? We need the pressure of those situations to help mold and shape our character. Just like a blacksmith must forge his metals in the fire to create the desired shape, so must we be forged through the competitive environments we experience. However, the key is to have blacksmiths (parents and coaches) who are forging strengths of character in our children rather than simply teaching them that winning on the scoreboard will make them happy and take all their problems away.

Responding to a Loss

It is also important to remember the competitive pressure should stop when the final buzzer sounds. A coach can use an after action review with his team in the locker room to analyze what went well, what areas need improvement, and what actions steps they need to take in the future. This time in the locker room is a time for teaching, not for criticizing or blaming.

At the same time, the ride home is an opportunity for parents to show their unconditional love for their children. Even if there was an issue which needs addressing, like poor body language, it could often wait until the next day. I once had a player tell me that even when he played well he usually did not want to talk about the game immediately afterward with his parents. Creating an environment where kids are allowed to decompress after a game can be a key to a successful parent-child relationship.

NBA basketball coach Brad Stevens once said how we handle our biggest defeats and our biggest wins are both true signs of our character.[3] This principle is maybe one of the greatest lessons I have tried to embrace throughout my coaching journey. I was always pretty good at staying humble when we won. I enjoyed the wins, but I attempted not to let them make me feel like I was on top of a mountain. However, I often allowed the losses to affect my mood, and sometimes it changed how I treated other people, especially my family and my players.

As I began to become more aware of this and was intentional about my mood after losses, I started to feel like I was doing something wrong if I was not depressed after we lost. I believe society has conditioned us to think we should mope around and pout if we lose because it shows how much we want to win. It is okay to be disappointed, especially if we gave our best effort and prepared as best we could, but it cannot affect our attitude or how we treat people. If we have the perspective to always learn and grow and move forward in a positive direction, then doesn't that show how much we want to win?

Sometimes people do not work very hard and prepare, but then are upset by the results. Sometimes people work hard when they think they have a chance to win on the scoreboard, but after things do not go their way, they stop putting forth their best effort. How do we expect to bounce back from a loss or get out of a slump if we let the results dictate our level of energy and commitment?

This situation is the reason legendary basketball coach John Wooden did not like his players to play with emotion, but preferred for them to play with an increasing level of intensity.[4] If we play with emotion the highs will feel great, and the lows will feel terrible, and we will be on an emotional rollercoaster.

So how do we stay off that rollercoaster? Play for the love of the game, don't put our value in outcomes and focus on the process of improving a little bit each day without comparing ourselves to others so we can enjoy the journey!

CHAPTER 2

Would You Rather...?

Our eight-year-old son came home from school one day and said they had completed an activity called "Would you rather...?" The question that day was, "Would you rather...play the game knowing that you will lose every time or not play the game at all?" I asked him what his answer was, and I was proud that he had the correct answer.

The internal benefits of playing a sport go far beyond the external rewards incurred by the final score on the scoreboard. But those internal benefits cannot be earned without taking advantage of the opportunity to play the game and understanding that the power is in the process.

When I was growing up one of my friends was a boy named Jake who lived down the street and was three years older than me. Some days I was at Jake's house all day and would only go home at meal times.

We played all kinds of sports, and we often made up our own versions of those sports because it was just the two of us. Football was often taking turns running pass patterns...sprint to the pine tree and then make a 45 degree cut to the left! Baseball was played one on one with a whiffle ball, a tree for first base, a rose bush for second base and a well cap for third base. Unfortunately, the flagpole in left-center field was not padded. We played basketball on a gravel driveway and, when it was too hot or cold, it was ping pong or pool in the basement.

Occasionally, I would get mad about something and go home. Later on, or the next day, I would be back. Not because I wanted to win, but because I loved to play and I loved to be with my friend. Lucky for me, Jake didn't mind and we picked right up where we left off.

I didn't start playing organized baseball until I was eight years old and basketball and flag football were around the same time. I would call myself a "competitive" person. I was always giving my best effort and trying to win, but I would say during grade school my teams lost more games than they won. However, losing never deterred me from wanting to play the game and I knew from playing with Jake that the more I practiced, the better I got.

Gaining the Edge

Frosty Westering talked about competing and being competitive in his book, *The Strange Secret of the Big Time*. He explained that one side of the coin (we will call it "tails") is competing against others and trying to be THE best. This type of competition often makes people frustrated because they are constantly comparing themselves to others.[1]

The other side of the coin (we will call it "heads") is competing against ourselves to be OUR best.[2] This perspective is great, but people often use this as a crutch and say, "Well I gave it my best," and they want to stop there. Frosty said that the competitive edge is not on either side of the coin, heads or tails, like we normally think. Instead, it is the third side of the coin, which is THE EDGE of the coin.

The edge is giving it our BEST SHOT. Giving it our best shot is not a singular occurrence; it is a process. It is continually striving to reach our best as we continue to reload, aim, and fire no matter what happens.[3] Giving it our best shot is playing the game with all our heart even though we know we may lose because we love the game and we know it is transforming us into a better person.

I find it interesting when people are in the midst of a losing streak or are having a season with many losses, and they say, "It is just so hard to lose game after game." One of my favorite authors, Jon Gordon, said that we don't get burned out because of what we do, but rather because we forget WHY we do what we do.[4] Why did we start playing sports when we were young? Was it so we could collect a bunch of trophies or was it because it was a fun experience and we enjoyed the relationships we developed?

It is possible that in some instances we start organized sports when kids are too young, and from the beginning, we are counting wins and losses before they can develop a genuine love for playing the game and competing to give it their best shot. We think we are making our kids more competitive when in reality we are replacing the internal motivation of the joy of playing with the external motivation of winning. Most people who are motivated externally are not going to maintain their motivation consistently over the long term. You can spot a person who is motivated externally because their effort level is like a roller coaster. They are the ones who are likely to say if they cannot get the reward then there is no point in competing.

According to John Maxwell, we need to follow the Law of Process and build our legacy one day at a time.[5] There are no shortcuts or get-rich-quick schemes. Whether we are talking about the skills of being a professional athlete or a concert pianist, or whether we are talking about the values of being a leader of character, we must build our house one brick at a time. Houses that are built too quickly often do not have the foundation or structure to withstand the forces of nature. We must be faithful in doing the small things without a desire to see the external rewards of our efforts. Instead, we should be alert for the internal rewards that we are collecting as part of the process.

Lag Time

One of the most challenging aspects of giving it our best shot time after time is we often do not see the fruits of our labor right away. We adjust our swing and expect to hit a home run the next day. We run some extra sprints and expect to win the next race. However, there is often lag time involved.[6] The improvement we make in our training today may not affect the results until next week, or next month, or next year. When we are training for excellence (to be the best we can be), we must remember that all improvements will pay off at some point, unless we quit before the improvement manifests itself. So even if we are losing, we can be making giant strides that will one day reveal themselves in improved results.

A great example of lag time and waiting for results to pay off is the story of Jason McElwain. Jason, also known as "J-Mac", was a manager on the Greece Athena (New York) High School basketball team. Jason has autism and every year he was cut from his high school team. However, "J-Mac" had a passion for basketball that was infectious and thanks to his coach, Jim Johnson, he could be a vital part of the team as the manager. He was at every practice, loved to talk basketball, and often accompanied Coach Johnson on scouting trips.

J-Mac regularly played in pick-up games at the local YMCA and even played in summer leagues with the Athena team. Even after being cut and asked to be the manager, he showed extreme loyalty and always put the team first. Coach Johnson rewarded Jason with the opportunity to dress for one varsity game during his senior season. On February 15th, 2006 J-Mac had his one shining moment as he scored 20 points in the final three minutes and 11 seconds of the senior night game amid an exuberant atmosphere of teammates and fans.[7]

What part of J-Mac's training and practice led to his historic night? It is hard to pinpoint, but it is reasonably easy to see it would not have happened if he had quit after being cut. It was a passion and a love for the game of basketball that drove J-Mac to rise above all the adversity in his life. He kept practicing and playing for years without seeing any external results until everything came together at the right time.

One of the best ways to overcome the urge to quit during lag time is to have intentness. John Wooden described intentness as the "ability to resist temptation and stay the course". Intentness is like determination and persistence; it does not involve wanting something, but instead it means to keep working at something consistently for a long time.[8] Every person runs a different race in life, and we cannot get caught up comparing our timeline to someone else's. If we show up every day and do the work, we will put ourselves in a position to reap results, but we cannot become frustrated based on when we think they should happen. And while we are working with intentness we might find that we accrue some benefits that are even more important.

Internal Rewards

Those improved results we are searching for may come in the form of external results of physical skill development, or they may come in the form of internal results of character development. If we are looking for it, mistakes and failures can create the perfect moment to reveal or develop character skills like resiliency, perseverance, and resourcefulness. When someone does something that we feel is unfair (like being cut from a team), we can use that opportunity to show integrity, humility, and respect. And the best thing about character skill development is there does not have to be any lag time. At any time, we have the opportunity to develop these skills. Yes, sometimes it does take a process to develop character, but the opportunities to contribute to that process are found in every situation in our lives.

I don't remember the score of those games we played back as kids in Jake's yard, but I developed a love for sports and learned how to give it my best shot. Just like J-Mac, it was those internal motivations that allowed me to play Division II college basketball for four years as a walk-on. It was that training ground for developing my internal motivation as a kid that helped me make it through those four years without giving up. After averaging just over two points per game in my college career, I scored a career-high 16 points on Senior Day during our final home game. It was a neat experience to have four years of training pay off with an external reward, but the internal rewards that I collected over those four years have been far more valuable throughout my life.

Former NFL player Mike Singletary said, "You know what my favorite part of the game is? The opportunity to play." I'm glad my son agrees with him because without the opportunity to play we will miss out on the internal rewards that are available.

.

CHAPTER 3

Reveal Our Greatness

Sometimes when we get a promotion or move into a new position, we think we have to change because people are now expecting more out of us, but that can often take away our ability to enjoy our journey. When I accepted the job as the varsity basketball coach at New Berlin High School in early August of 2007, I did not have the luxury of working with the team at all during the summer. I had to rely on information provided by our assistant coach, and I would have two weeks of practice before playing five games in eight days as part of our season-opening Thanksgiving tournament.

In other words, I had a short amount of time to evaluate our team and get to know them. For some players, this can be good as it can provide a fresh start and clean slate. For others, it may cause some anxiety to perform immediately and impress the new coach. Some of our favorite stories involve someone who rises above adversity and dares to reveal the greatness they have inside of them. Eventually, I would learn that by staying true to our character the people who matter to us will appreciate us for who we are.

I usually do not like to single out players, but I would like to share with you the story of Matt Brown, a.k.a "Brownie". We had four seniors on the roster, and only two of them were playing their fourth year in the basketball program. Brownie was one of those fourth-year seniors, and he had some of the most unfundamental shooting mechanics I have ever seen.

One of my first memories of Brownie was at practice during the first week of the season when we were doing partner shooting drills. He was shooting on a side basket where the 3-point line was not marked but he was probably behind where it would have been. I saw him miss a couple of shots in a row and told him to move in because he was out of his range. He looked at me like I was crazy and said, "I'm a 3-point shooter." I just thought, "Okay we'll see about that."

As I came to find out, Brownie's shooting technique was so famous it had developed a moniker, "The Diamond Cutter." He shot the ball with two hands by bringing the ball up just over his forehead and then slinging it toward the basket. I'm sure you have probably made a diamond shape with your hands before using your thumbs and index fingers. That is how Brownie held the ball when he shot it. I was taught to catch a football that way but never to shoot a basketball that way.

I developed a philosophy that I was not going to make significant overhauls to the shooting technique of a player, especially during the season. I was a pretty good high school shooter, but it took me nearly four years of college basketball to become a consistently good shooter.

I spent many, many hours in the offseason working on my form and technique and I knew that unless a player was going to commit a considerable amount of time to improve their shot, I was going to do more harm than good by making them change and giving them too much to think about. In addition, it will not work if the player is unwilling to change and most players don't like to change their shot because it is uncomfortable. This feeling causes them to miss more for some time until they become more comfortable with the form. Thus, the Diamond Cutter remained.

Defining Roles

During the first two weeks of the season, I sat down with each player individually and talked about their goals for the season and where I saw their role on the team at that time. I strove to be honest and realistic with the players, while also showing them that things could always change and there was still room for growth and improvement.

I still remember the spot in the bleachers where we were sitting when I had my meeting with Brownie. I don't recollect everything that was said, but I remember telling him that, at that time, he was probably not going to be in the regular rotation and I was not sure how much playing time he would get. His verbatim response was, "That's fine. I just enjoy being part of the team."

WOW! No rolling his eyes. No huffing and puffing. I did not receive a phone call, e-mail, or get notified there was a Facebook discussion over what I said. But that is not the best part. The best part is how the rest of the story turns out.

We had a rough start to the year in terms of wins and losses. Overall, the kids were working hard and trying to adjust to our new standards. Not only were we changing what we did on the basketball court, but we were changing what it meant to be a basketball player in our program off the court as well. Some kids adjusted well and met expectations, and some struggled to understand that how you do something is how you do everything.

I had a list of prescribed rules and consequences that I had been following, but two of the players seemed to be pushing the envelope quite a bit. During a pre-game discussion in the locker room in December, I informed the team these two players (one was a starter, and the other was one of the first subs off the bench normally) would not start and would not be playing in the first half of the game. I told the team exactly what the players had done and why they would not be playing the first half.

I also explained I was taking the opportunity to start two players who had not received much playing time so far but had been working their tails off and doing everything we asked of them, one of them being Brownie. I explained that the two players who were sitting out the first half would have an opportunity to play in the second half.

Brownie was impressive. Although he did not score a ton of points, his energy, enthusiasm, and toughness provided a spark that you could feel affected the whole team. After trailing the entire game but staying within striking distance, we were in a position to take the lead with less than 30 seconds to go as we had possession of the ball. We called a play for one of the players who had sat out the first half, and it worked beautifully as the player made a great move to score. He then stole the inbounds pass to negate the opponent's opportunity to retake the lead.

Message sent. Message received.

The beauty is not the fact that we won the game, but in how we won the game. The reason we won the game is not due to the boundaries I enforced. Rather, the reason we won the game was due to the character of the players and how they collectively responded when challenged. Winning is not valuable unless you put an investment of character into it.

I have always been a follower of John Wooden and his philosophies, which include the Pyramid of Success that he created to detail the characteristics he believed were necessary to succeed in all aspects of life. Wooden explained that the Pyramid was not designed as a formula to produce championships; rather, its purpose was to help each member of a team reach excellence (his or her full potential). Winning a game or a championship was simply a by-product.[1] That game we won during my first season is a prime example of winning a game as a result of living the characteristics of excellence.

Does that mean then when you win a game you have character and when you lose you don't? There are many factors involved in the outcome of a game and playing with enthusiasm, poise, and confidence (characteristics of the Pyramid) every time will give you a better chance at winning, but it does not guarantee it. However, the result on the scoreboard does not mean you are not winning in your quest to be the person you want to be. In addition, you can meet victory humbly and defeat with an attitude of learning and growth.

Be So Great a Role Cannot Hold You Back

Brownie is a tremendous example of embracing a role and helping teammates improve while preparing for an opportunity. He took full advantage of his opportunity and became a starter for a large part of the season. Brownie's hustle and determination became a staple of our team during that time, and The Diamond Cutter came through with some big baskets as well.

Brownie's consistent play and leadership were a big part of our turnaround. He is a shining example of someone who does their work and goes about their business without any fanfare. He is committed, loyal, dependable and takes significant pride in everything he does.

A few years after graduating we were looking for a 7th-grade basketball coach and Brownie stepped in to help. A couple of years later he moved up and became our freshmen basketball coach, a position he stayed in for the next four years until my tenure was over. Brownie was pretty green with many of our strategies, but he was open to learning. He wanted to help our kids learn the same lessons he learned.

During that time Brownie had been working for several years as a member of the maintenance staff. An opportunity arose, and he earned the position as head of maintenance for the entire junior high and high school building at the age of 22 years old. If you live with character and strive for excellence in all you do opportunities will often find you.

Brownie was by my side at the school board meeting when I was fired as the head basketball coach after nine seasons at New Berlin. He told me that, besides his parents, I was most responsible for helping him develop his work ethic. Sure, I was happy when we won some of those games Brownie's senior year, but that is nothing compared to the pride I felt in my heart when he told me that. Brownie taught me that if we stick with it and stay true to our character we will reveal the greatness within us and people will eventually realize and appreciate what we have to offer.

Thank you Brownie for everything you did to help me, but most importantly thank you for being who you are!

CHAPTER 4

Be Positive

"C'mon Hannah…"

"We are going to be late…"

"If you don't get dressed right now…"

There is a gap in every childhood between when we rely on our parents to get us dressed because we cannot do it and when we can get ourselves dressed and ready for the day independently. Not too long ago I was living in that gap with our daughter. As a parent, we have the choice to continue to do things for our child or help them learn how to do them on their own. In many of these situations, there will come the point where we will have to decide between results and relationships. Being positive means taking action and using words to encourage the heart of those we lead so that we can create an environment that builds strong relationships.

As anyone with children can relate, getting our children out of bed and ready for the day can be one of the most challenging tasks in our life. More than college final exams, more than negotiating with a car salesperson, more than day-after-Thanksgiving shopping, this experience can test our patience, our will, and our belief in ourselves.

I have learned that getting negative is rarely the best way. Now, negativity may still get us to our destination of having our child ready for the day, but the path of destruction we leave behind can make us question whether we are even fit to be a parent.

As the daily chore of getting Hannah ready for the day became more and more frustrating, I found my fuse getting shorter and shorter. It became easier and easier to lose my cool, raise my voice, and threaten. While I may have reached the result that I wanted, Hannah was dressed, had her teeth brushed, and hair combed, I did not feel right once the adrenaline drained out of my body, and I certainly felt terrible about the tears streaming down her face.

A Look in the Mirror

So I decided some things (or someone) had to change.

First, I decided I would start waking Hannah up earlier to give us more time in case she was uncooperative, or there were reasons for a delay. Second, I decided I needed to be more energetic and try to use laughter to help ease the transition. Third, I decided to review the routine with her the night before, including what I expected her to do to cooperate and why it was important to get ready on time.

Finally, I decided that I needed to remember what was most important. The fact that her clothes did not match was NOT most important. The fact that she wanted to wear the same two or three outfits all the time was NOT most important.

There were some boundaries like making sure our clothes were appropriate for the weather, but how many lives have been affected by the clothing styles worn by a 4-year-old?

One of the most significant ways to build confidence in a relationship is to have the strength to admit when we are wrong. When we don't want to admit our mistake or don't want to be held accountable for our actions, then we are considered arrogant and untrustworthy.[1] And without trust, the relationship will not have any strength.

What was the best way for me to admit I was wrong? It was to change my behavior. Sure, it is essential to apologize and communicate with someone when we make a mistake, but changing our behavior is the best way to show we are indeed holding ourselves accountable to learn from our mistakes and use them to become better people.

It is not just about having a positive mindset. It is about taking positive action to help avoid as many pitfalls as possible. It is about hoping for the best but being prepared to meet the worst head-on. It is about remembering that making it to the destination is not worth ruining relationships in the process.

The Power of Words

Words can inspire. Words can empower. Words can also tear down and damage lives.

The experience of a child playing sports is mainly made up of interactions with teammates, coaches, and parents. While people outside of that circle may judge us based on the results they see in the newspaper, we cannot fool the people inside the circle.

The relationships, far more than the wins and losses, are what a person will remember about their athletic experience. We build relationships on communication made up of the words we use. And no amount of success on the scoreboard can overcome a coach or parent who uses the power of their words to degrade and demean.

In *The Four Agreements*, Don Miguel Ruiz stated, "The word is a force; it is the power you have to express and communicate, to think, and thereby to create the events in your life."[2] As a coach, I have not been perfect, and there were players who I did not do a good enough job communicating with. Those are the things that sting way more than losing games. The times I did not choose to use encouraging words were usually the result of my focus on the scoreboard and when I felt the result in the win-loss column would impact my value and identity.

Jim Kouzes and Barry Posner have spent years studying the behavior of great leaders, and they have subsequently created The Leadership Challenge, which they based on five core practices: Model the Way, Inspire a Shared Vision, Challenge the Process, Enable Others to Act, and Encourage the Heart.[3] Each of these methods requires some form of communication, but encouraging the heart is most definitely achieved through words.

Will we get better results on the scoreboard if, as parents and coaches, we encourage the heart of our children and players? Maybe, maybe not. But I guarantee we will get better results in our relationships. Imagine if encouraging the heart was the measuring stick surrounding our leadership rather than external results!

It is an awesome feeling to walk downstairs with Hannah experiencing a great start to our day. We still have setbacks, but I'm glad I learned to take positive action and use the power of words to put relationships before results. We can still get results, but those that come as the product of nurturing relationships are much sweeter!

CHAPTER 5

Let the Score Take Care of Itself

We like to be in control. We want to think we can affect people and the situations in which we are involved. We base part of our American culture on this idea that we have created so many things and that we can do anything we set our minds to. Many other cultures of the world focus more on the environment and context of a situation, while in America we tend to focus on the individual people and the role they played in that situation. A true leader will help create the right conditions for success and allow individuals to reveal their greatness by experiencing success from within.

One of my biggest coaching influences is a wonderful person named Sean Taylor. After four years of attending Quincy University in Quincy, Illinois and playing basketball,

I completed my student teaching at Quincy Junior High School and was a volunteer assistant coach at QU. I was then offered a full-time teaching job at the junior high, and I approached Coach Taylor, who was the Quincy High School varsity coach, one day and inquired if he had coaching positions open in the basketball program. Like many great mentors, Coach Taylor often believed in me more than I believed in myself.

I coached 7th grade basketball the first year and then worked with the same awesome group of kids the next year in 8th grade. The following year I was set to move up with that same group again and coach the freshmen, but during the summer, Coach Taylor asked me if I wanted to be the varsity assistant. It was my dream to be a head coach, and I jumped at the chance. For those of you that are not familiar with Quincy High School, they have the fourth most wins for a boys high school basketball program in the nation. Their gym and locker rooms are superior to many at the college level, and they have quite a following from the community.

At some point during that season Coach Taylor asked me, "Do you ever have trouble sleeping the night before a game?"

My answer was, "Not as an assistant coach."

Now for those that know me, I do not usually have a hard time falling asleep. But after being a head coach, yes there were times I had trouble falling asleep. So what is the difference? Could it be that we tie the identity of the head coach to the results, the team's win-loss record? Obviously, the head coach is the head coach who makes the final decisions, but the question is, does the head coach have control over the results?

Focus on the Process

In his book *Eleven Rings: The Soul of Success*, legendary NBA coach Phil Jackson said, "The most we can hope for is to create the best possible conditions for success, then let go of the outcome. The ride is a lot more fun that way."[1] So, according to Jackson, the head coach is responsible for creating the best possible conditions for success, but not the outcome.

Long-time NFL coach and winner of three Super Bowls with the San Francisco 49ers, Bill Walsh, agreed with Jackson. He said there is no guarantee or ultimate formula for success. The key is to create an environment with high standards, get the right people on board, and let the score take care of itself.[2] It is incredible that coaches of professional sports, where it is a business based on winning and losing, and millions of dollars are involved, can have that belief. Perhaps after having been on the other side of winning championships, they understand it is not a golden ticket that brings us happiness for the rest of our lives.

In an interview with Brett Ledbetter at the What Drives Winning Conference in 2015, NBA Coach Billy Donovan talked about the myth that a player or a coach can "will" something to happen in an athletic contest. Sometimes announcers will talk about how someone is "willing" the ball into the basket or "willing" their team to victory. If this is possible, then why are they not undefeated? Do they just decide to "will" their team to victory on some nights and not on others?[3] If we honestly had control over the results, then we would all be undefeated. The truth is we do not have control over the results. We have control over the process. And character influences that process.

When we talk about character education or character development, many people get defensive because they think we are judging people and putting them either in the category of good character or bad character. This is not true. We are talking about everyone improving and developing their character no matter where they are. We are not comparing anyone to anyone else, but we focus relentlessly on improving our perspective to make right decisions. Brett Ledbetter calls these attributes "skills" because we can develop them; they are not fixed at birth.

Character Skills

World-renowned performance psychologist Jim Loehr places character skills in two categories: performance skills and moral skills. Performance skills, including motivation, focus, and resilience, govern a person's relationship with himself or herself and have an impact on performance in athletics or other work capacities. Moral skills, including honesty, respect, and trustworthiness, govern a person's relationship with other human beings and have an impact on those human interactions.[4]

Loehr emphasized that moral character skills must always take precedence over performance character skills. Why? Because who we are as a person and how we treat others is far more critical than what we accomplish on the court or field. Also, people who are happier, more stable human beings perform at a higher level because they are emotionally and mentally free to play with total release.[5]

Total release is playing without a fear of failure because we know that failure does not define us. Total release is focusing on the process and leaning on the many hours of training that we have put into an activity. Total release is playing for the love of the game. And love is not motivated by the prospect of getting something in return.

Playing with total release is like running with the wind at our back. We don't have to expend as much energy, and it feels like a higher power is helping push us along. We are not focused on anyone else in the race but enjoy the physiological and psychological benefits of the activity itself. Playing with the pressure to win is like running into the wind. We may still win the race, but we are going to expend significant energy in the process. We will have to put our head down and fight the conditions while we miss out on the surrounding beauty.

Eventually, the wind (the pressure to win) is going to wear us down. We may start to lose games and fall more behind in the race, and the wind is going to feel even stronger than it did before and make us want to quit. If we can run with the wind at our back, we can stay refreshed and energized.

Now, is a coach, or any person for that matter, able to change the character of his players or any human beings? Absolutely not! The change must occur from the inside-out in each person. "That's why at the start of every season I always encouraged players to focus on the journey rather than the goal. What matters most is playing the game the right way and having the courage to grow, as human beings as well as basketball players. When you do that, the ring takes care of itself," said Phil Jackson.[6] Again, a coach must create the right conditions for physical skill development in their particular sport, but also in character development, which can make them a better player, but more importantly a better person.

If I had to go back and respond to Coach Taylor's question again, I would point him to the wise words of Phil Jackson, "As a leader your job is to do everything in your power to create the perfect conditions for success by benching your ego and inspiring your team to play the game the right way. But at some point, you need to let go and turn yourself over to the basketball gods. The soul of success is surrendering to what is."[7] As parents and coaches, we can sleep well at night when we know we created an environment for our children and players to relentlessly pursue being the best human being they are capable of becoming.

CHAPTER 6

I Love Watching You Play

A few years ago I came across a TED talk with John O'Sullivan from Changing the Game Project[1] with a message that has had a profound impact on me as a parent.

I was never an over-the-top parent who made a scene at games, but before watching the video, I would sometimes get frustrated watching our kids play and say stuff to them about their effort and attitude during the game. I realized that there are times and places to address some of these issues, but it should always be well after the game is over and after I have told them, "I love watching you play." Telling our children we love watching them play is the foundation we must establish to lead effectively as parents.

When I first started telling our kids this, it felt awkward. Especially when their effort was maybe not good, or they weren't precisely focused on the game. However, I believe as I started doing it more, it has empowered our kids to give their best because they know they have our love and support no matter how they perform.

My wife, Sarah, is tremendous at telling our kids that she loves watching them play, and although I sometimes still get frustrated, her consistency is a good reminder that these five words can make a huge difference with our kids.

What Did You Learn?

Our oldest son, Nathan, loves to play soccer. I had never played on a soccer team growing up, and my wife played youth soccer just a couple of years. When Nathan was six years old, he was asked to play on a soccer team because they needed another player.

I still remember Nathan walking up to one of the practices the first year dribbling the soccer ball like a basketball. The coach said to me, "I'm sorry, but he is totally going to be a basketball player. I'm not sure about soccer." He was not condescending or mean, but I have often thought about that moment and wondered if people think at six years old it is determined what type of athlete someone is going to be and what sports they will play?

Fast forward five years and Nathan was on a different soccer team with kids he had never played with before.

They had a good season and were the #1 seed in the end-of-season tournament. After winning their first game, they were playing in the semifinals against a team they had beaten previously.

Nathan was the team's top goal scorer and played offense about 90% of the time, but in the second half of the game, the coach moved him to defense even though they were behind on the scoreboard and needed to score. I simply watched to see how Nathan would handle it.

We ended up losing, and after telling Nathan that I loved watching him play, I asked him what he learned that day. He responded that he learned he could play a different position on defense and still do a good job and help his team. That is a lesson that will benefit Nathan far more than merely winning that game and not taking a lesson from it.

Then, as we were walking to our car, the wife of Nathan's coach stopped us and said Nathan was an excellent athlete and a good soccer player but that he was an even better person. She said that she watched how he interacted with his teammates and the opponents and that he was so mature and had such good sportsmanship.

Which Lessons Are We Teaching?

I don't tell this story to brag about my son. Instead, I want to point out that what we emphasize is what we will get. If our perspective is to learn valuable lessons from our sports experience, then that is what we are going to get. If our perspective is that winning is everything and that second place is the first loser, then that is what we are going to get. Dr. Carol Dweck has spent years researching people's mindsets and the impact of those mindsets on performance. She has concluded growth-minded people can value the activity they participate in no matter the outcome.[2] In other words, play for the love of the game and enjoy a victory, but find value in competing in a win or a loss.

Do you think Nathan is less likely to win his next game because he was not pouting and upset they lost the game? On the contrary, I think Nathan is more likely to have a favorable impact on the next game due to his perspective. And no matter the outcome of that next game, I can guarantee that there will be a lesson in it to help him. We can learn when we win and we can learn when we lose...if we have the proper perspective.

We need to tell our kids we love watching them play and help them learn valuable lessons that they can take with them for the rest of their lives. Because, in reality, they are always learning. The question is, "Which lessons are we teaching?"

Defining Success

I think we need to begin making a clear distinction between two common words: success and achievement.

Let's begin with the dictionary definition of each. The dictionary defines success as the favorable or prosperous termination of attempts or endeavors; the accomplishment of one's goals. It also describes success as the attainment of wealth, position, honors, or the like.[3] Meanwhile, the dictionary defines achievement as something accomplished, especially by superior ability, special effort, or great courage; a great or heroic deed.[4]

The key word from the definition of success I would like to look at is termination. According to this definition, we can only attain success at the end of the race or the top of the mountain. This description says we are not truly successful until we have obtained something that the world deems of value. A vital point here is the item of value is often something external or materialistic, like money, a job title, or a trophy. The scary part is these items of value can be taken away or disappear quickly, and even the feelings of pride that accompany them are often ephemeral.

Two of my mentors had different ideas about what success really means. John Wooden penned his own definition of success. "Success is peace of mind, which is a direct result of self-satisfaction in knowing you did the best to become the best you are capable of becoming."[5] As we break down that definition, we see the determination of success goes from external to internal, and the responsibility for that decision goes from society to the individual.

Also, Coach Wooden was concerned with fulfilling one's potential or capabilities. At first glance, we might think this is congruent with accomplishing one's goals, as the dictionary says. However, several issues exist with the goal theory. We can set goals that are easily attainable, thereby claiming success without stretching ourselves to our full potential. At the same time, a goal can be unrealistic and cause us to give up because we believe we are a failure by not claiming those external rewards. And worst of all, we often let others set our goals for us, and we end up chasing "success" to please others.

Another coach who had a different model of success was Frosty Westering. Frosty declared many people in society believe in the dictionary definition of success and travel on the "Road to Success." Again, according to this philosophy, we must reach a destination before being crowned with success. Conversely, Frosty believed in traveling on the "Success Road." On the Success Road, we focus on our best self. We can experience success daily because we are in control of our effort. Frosty's philosophy embodied the principle that the real measure of a person is what he or she can do compared to their best self, rather than what they can do compared to others.[6] As we have discussed previously, the way to reach our best self is to give it our best shot on a continual basis. For both John Wooden and Frosty Westering, success is internal and can only truly be determined by the person.

Switching gears back to the definition of achievement, we see it also involves an outcome because we must accomplish something. The interesting thing about this definition is it explains what is needed in the process to get to the end of the race or the top of the mountain. The dictionary points to effort and courage and even goes so far as to use the term "heroic". In other words, it takes specific character skills, and the actions resulting from those character skills, to get to that endpoint and experience achievement.

I would like to make it clear that there is nothing wrong with achievement. The act of earning money, attaining a particular job, or winning a trophy are not things that we should look at with disgust. However, we can experience those achievements and still not be successful. And experiencing those results does not give us the right to break the rules or treat people poorly. Achievements are achievements, but they are external, and they do not impact the value (positively or negatively) and self-worth of individual human beings. There is a vast difference between a DESIRE to win and a NEED to win. As John Wooden and Frosty Westering taught us, winning (achievement) is a by-product of real success. The value of those achievements come from the deposits of character we make in the process of reaching for them.

Redefining Success for Ourselves

In 2013, I began a Master of Arts in Education program with an emphasis in Coaching through Greenville College. This experience catapulted my drive for personal transformation. I had always been a student of John Wooden, but that program introduced me to Frosty Westering as well as other mentors I follow. Through that course of study I created my own definition of success:

> *"Success is the process of striving to achieve excellence, which is living up to our full potential. This journey involves giving it our best shot each day in order to improve in body, mind, and soul."*

True success can often lead to achievement, but the two are not always connected. The focus must be on the process, and that process must entail working to become the best version of ourselves. Telling our children we love watching them play creates the foundation to help them define their own success in their quest for excellence. These five words can be the key to unlocking our greatest potential in the relationship with our children and change our lives forever.

Chapter 7

The Coach is the Student

"Do you even want to win?"

That was the thought in my mind as I entered the locker room. We were in the middle of a season in which we would only win two games, and we had just lost a game that we had been leading almost the whole way.

Every situation provides an opportunity to make a long-term impact on those we lead. When we let the scoreboard define our value, we tend to blame others and make excuses. However, when we focus on the lessons we can learn, we can make adjustments to keep gaining forward progress. Those adjustments may seem insignificant at the moment, but they can have a tremendous impact over time.

As I walked into the locker room that night with my assistant coach, I heard the players laughing and joking about a situation in the game where one of the opposing players received a technical.

The thought in my head came out of my mouth, "Do you even want to win? I mean we just lost a game that we should have won and you guys are joking around about someone from the other team getting a technical?"

After a few moments of silence, one of the players responded, "Maybe that is how we deal with it."

Another player chimed in, "Maybe that is how we forget about it and move on."

Boom! I have no idea what I said in the locker room after that because those statements were all I could think about. And it still impacts me to this day.

Next Play

Our children and players are not the only ones who should be learning from every competitive experience we have. If we have the right perspective, we should be the ones learning first so we can be a better guide and mentor. And sometimes it is our kids that are teaching us the lessons. What if we repurposed the ride home so that, as parents and coaches, we could reflect on the lessons learned and then use those experiences the next day to help mentor our children and players? This change would help everyone move forward and make the next play.

I couldn't even tell you why we ended up losing the lead in that game. Did we miss some shots? Maybe. Did we make some unforced turnovers or commit some silly fouls? Maybe. Did the other team catch fire and start making shots they were missing earlier in the game? Maybe.

Did we give our best effort that night? Yeah, we did. Remember, a poor performance does not always mean a poor effort.

What would have been more productive in that situation? Many things.

Fellas, what did we do well tonight? What are some things we need to work on to improve? Give me some ideas of what we can do at practice tomorrow to move us toward where we want to be.

Focusing on the next play is a concept that Duke University Men's Basketball Coach Mike Krzyzewski learned during his time at West Point.[1] This principle transcends sports and can help us in all areas of our lives. Accept what happened, celebrate the positives, identify areas for improvement, and decide on a solution to move forward; make the next play.

Were we not winning more games simply because we didn't want to win bad enough? Did we not have enough goals focused on winning that would motivate the kids to try harder? I came across an article about a high school coach who resigned after 20 seasons, the final 14 of which were at the same school, to focus on his family. I do not know what his overall coaching record was, but he had at least four 20-win seasons and won at least one Regional championship. His athletic director had the following to say about him:

> *"The thing about John was that winning wasn't the most important thing. He wanted to mold the kids into better people. He cared so much about the kids. That said, I knew we would never be outcoached and that the kids would go through a wall for him."*[2]

Focusing on the results, moping around, and telling everyone how bad we want to win does not make us more competitive. It is possible to focus on developing people, rather than winning, but still work hard to teach the game and prepare our players and win games as a by-product. When we are focused on reaching excellence, then we can see the big picture of the journey we are on, and we can have the proper perspective that keeps us moving forward.

Transactional vs. Transformational

A few years after that incident in the locker room I enrolled in the Master's program at Greenville College. One of the required texts to read was *InSideOut Coaching: How Sports Can Transform Lives* by former NFL player Joe Ehrmann. In the book, Ehrmann discussed the difference between transactional coaches and transformational coaches. Transactional coaches are "the kind of coaches who use players as tools to meet their personal needs for validation, status, and identity." Meanwhile, transformational coaches "use their coaching platform to impart life-changing messages."[3]

In the competitive environment of sports, it is easy to lose our perspective and get caught up in the idea that if we can just win it will make us better people and change our lives. In *The Only Way to Win*, performance psychologist Jim Loehr made it clear that success does not breed happiness. In reality, the opposite is true in that happiness often breeds success.[4] If we want to get the order right, we have to make people more important than results. Eddie Reese coached swimming and diving across four decades at the University of Texas and won numerous national championships. He once remarked he had no clue where any of his championship rings were. "I know what every kid did and how much they improved. Those are the things that matter. It's always about people," Reese stated.[5] The lessons we teach our children and players help them become better people more than their win-loss record as a player.

Transformational coaching and leadership are not easy. Many people don't want to do the difficult work of looking inside and acknowledging what they need to change to become the best person they can be. As a transformational coach, the first thing I had to do was start looking inside myself and trying to understand why I coached the way I coached.

I realized it was my vision to be a transformational coach, and in many ways I was, but there were also times when I became transactional. It is a natural human tendency to want to be liked and to want people to think well of you. When you are losing and people start looking at you differently, and the parents of the players won't make eye contact with you, or they send degrading texts and e-mails it takes a tremendous amount of courage to rise above that. In my heart, I knew that we didn't have to win to prove we were successful, but I conformed to the expectations of society and became frustrated when we were losing. I thought if we would just win more games it would change the way people perceived me and treated me.

Winning Changes Everything...

The year after the incident in the locker room we increased our number of wins by 12 and won 14 games and played in the regional championship game for the first time in seven years. The following year we won 15 games and won the school's first regional championship in 18 years. I thought we had turned the corner and the culture we had established was finally starting to pay off. We had an outstanding number of kids showing up to work on their skills before school during that spring, and we had a pretty good summer season. With three of our top six players from the previous year coming back expectations and excitement were high. But what can sometimes take years to build can be undone quickly.

We won five games that year, and three of them were during the last week of the season. We had five players suspended for the first seven games of the season for violating the athletic code of conduct. We had two key players miss over half the season due to injuries. And our attitudes, including mine, were not the best. I was ejected from a game early in the season for arguing with the referees and receiving two technical fouls. After running my sprints at the next practice, which was the team consequence for receiving a technical, and receiving a stern warning from my wife, I learned my lesson and have since not received a technical.

As I look back, I realized I was frustrated because after feeling like we had built so much momentum and moved things in the right direction it seemed like it was all crumbling apart. But maybe we had truly not changed the culture. Maybe people were pretending to buy into the culture because we were winning. Perhaps winning just covered up the perspectives that were part of the problem. As long as I could provide the transaction of creating temporary happiness as the coach who won more games, I would be able to survive.

...Except Winning Changes Nothing

Some people think success breeds success and, from the outside, this can often appear to be the case. But John Wooden said that success breeds satisfaction and satisfaction breeds failure.[6] Did we get complacent that year and think we were simply going to win games based on the regional championship we had won the previous year? Traditionally, I believe the teams I coached improved as the season progressed and this team showed that; once we overcame injuries and finally gelled together we won three of our five games in the last week of the season. But some of the parents who had supported me the year before when we won the regional championship, had jumped ship until I could prove I could win again.

John Wooden was the coach of a record 10 NCAA men's basketball national championship teams at UCLA. However, all 10 of the championships came in the last half of his 27-year coaching tenure. They did not win a national championship until Wooden's fifteenth year. In 1974, UCLA lost in the national semifinals after having won nine championships in the previous ten years. They came back to win another national title the next year in Wooden's last season. After that final championship game, a UCLA alumnus congratulated Wooden on the championship and said it was especially nice after he (Wooden) had let them down the previous year by not winning it.[7] If our value comes from winning then once we start winning, we have to keep winning, or we are not successful. Although Coach Wooden enjoyed the championships because of the character his players put into their preparation, he was just like Eddie Reese in that the ultimate satisfaction he gained from coaching was through the development of his players and the relationships he formed with them.

Many times we look at the result on the scoreboard and then use the outcome to justify whether a play or a decision during the game was the right one or the wrong one. But Mike Krzyzewski explained we can make a play that is the winning play at that moment, but it ends up not working, and we could lose the game. In *Leading With the Heart*, he related the story from the 1999 National Championship game when Trajan Langdon decided to drive to the basket and make a spin move, but he ended up traveling. Even though he turned the ball over and they ended up losing the game, Coach K said it was the winning thing to do at that moment in the game.[8]

We have to follow our heart and have the courage to make the decision that we feel is the right thing to do at that time and live with the result either way. That is trusting the process. That is striving to be the best we can be. That will help us bounce back and give our best shot the next time around. I encourage you to take the advice of Coach K and never allow losing a game to break your heart.[9] Because when we let results define us, it is impossible to bring out our best.

Authenticity

Five years after that incident in the locker room and three years after winning the regional championship, we lost another game that we had been leading and we "should" have won. Rather than complaining that we did not want to win bad enough, I shared the following message from long-time NCAA swimming coach Eddie Reese with the team: "The hardest skill to acquire...is the one where you compete all out, give it all you have, and you are still getting beat no matter what you do. When you have the killer instinct to fight through that, it is very special."[10] On the bus ride home after that game, the kids were laughing and joking and having a good time. I remembered the lesson I learned; maybe that was how they dealt with it and how they moved on, so I did not say anything. We played a game the next night and won. Was it due to my response to the game the night before? I have no idea, but my response to our loss the previous night was the winning play to make at that moment.

At the end of that season, I was fired from my position as the basketball coach for not winning enough games and being too focused on building character. It was interesting that the more I became courageous to speak about my mission to use basketball to teach about life, the more resistance I received. Brené Brown described authenticity as "willing to let go of who you think you should be in order to be who you are."[11] Even though it was a challenging situation to be ridiculed and rejected in my hometown, it has actually been a blessing. If I had remained in my position as the coach, I would have had to continue to endure a situation that hindered me from being my true and authentic self. And that would have been a far greater tragedy than actually being fired.

After I was fired, I received the following text message from Tyler, a former player who made one of those statements in the locker room after our frustrating loss five years earlier:

> *"Hey coach! My dad just told me the news this weekend about the school board's decision and I just thought it was important for me to tell you that even though we didn't have the most successful years together on varsity I do greatly value all of the lessons that came from going through that experience with you as my coach. I do believe that I am a better person and grew much more in areas I use every day because of the coach you were. So thank you for being the coach that you were. I was very proud to play under you."*

No, Tyler, THANK YOU for teaching me a lesson that I still use every day. Making small adjustments really can have a profound impact.

CHAPTER 8

Keep on Failing

We like to pass on traditions to our children. We teach them to root for the same sports teams as us. Many times our children end up working in the same professions or running the family business. But what we must realize is our children are also watching for how we respond to failure and what we can teach them. They are looking for someone to show them how to be a hero. Parents and coaches can create heroes by affirming the process it takes to achieve something and living the sermon they are trying to preach to their children and players.

For some of us, we encounter the circumstance where we coach our own children. When I am in these situations, I am conscientious of the dual role of being a coach and a parent. I try to coach them at practice and games and be a parent as soon as those structured times are over. Occasionally, they will ask me to work with them on some skill at home, and I am more than happy to spend that time with them.

I was coaching my son Jacob, who was nine years old at the time, on his basketball team. He was so excited because he is right-handed and he attempted to make a layup from the left side of the basket with his left hand. At practice, we worked on the proper footwork and using the appropriate hand from both sides of the basket. We even worked on the fundamentals of shooting a layup without a ball when we began. But as is often the case, kids will revert to what is most comfortable during the pressure of the games.

When Jacob attempted the left-hand layup and missed it, I made sure I got his attention and affirmed him for trying to do it the right way. After a couple more games and a few more attempts, he made a left-hand layup going full speed with someone right in front of him.

Affirm the Process

After the game as we drove home (and after I said I loved watching him play), I told Jacob that the reason he made that layup was because of all the other layups that he had the courage to attempt and miss. I could have just praised him and said, "Great job!" However, the real impact came by affirming the process it took to get there. He achieved something because he dared to leave his comfort zone and try something different. He also had the persistence to keep doing it, even though he didn't get it right the first time, or the second time, or the third time...

Keep on failing until we get it right. But we must have two things. First, we need to have the support and the mindset it is okay to fail as long as we are giving our best because that is how we learn and grow. And, we need to have the perseverance and tenacity to push through when it doesn't happen right away, when we want to blame others, and when everyone tells us to quit.

Mistakes, failures, or whatever we want to call them can be reasons to quit or they can be stepping stones to later achievements. In his book *The Obstacle is the Way*, Ryan Holiday vividly pointed out that every great individual has suffered setbacks. However, the greatest not only endure their obstacles but thrive because of them.[1] There is an opportunity in every difficulty and obstacles and failures are not merely something to endure, but they are present to teach us lessons and help us become stronger than before.

Does that mean we should go in with a mindset that we are going to lose? Absolutely not! We should believe every time we step in the arena it is possible for us to win, but mistakes and failures do not define us. They are simply a way for us to get out of our comfort zone and push the limits of what we think is possible.

Dr. Carol Dweck's mindsets confront obstacles in opposite ways. For the person with a fixed mindset, a mistake or an upcoming difficulty has the potential to expose them for not being perfect. Meanwhile, a person with a growth mindset will see a challenge as an opportunity to learn. Because for the growth mindset it is not so much about where we are right now, but what we are going to learn and who we are going to be as a result of the obstacles and errors we overcome.[2] Mistakes and failures can be the perfect opportunity for us to show the world what we have inside.

Living the Sermon

Once we break through that barrier of responding to failure and getting over it, we will see that we have the resilience and courage to rise above our obstacles and it will become easier as we move forward. Mike Krzyzewski sees losses and failures not only as opportunities to learn but ones to grow character as well.[3] Just like we enjoy reading stories or watching movies about the heroes who overcome adversity to reveal their greatness, we can start building our own story that we can refer back to and remind ourselves that we can be the hero. In fact, sometimes there are people close to us who are waiting for us to be the hero.

When we start to understand that overcoming mistakes and failures is not only for us, but could also be the inspiration that someone is looking for, it takes on a whole new meaning. As Branch Rickey told Jackie Robinson in the epic movie *42*, "You're the one living the sermon."[4] Our life, and how we respond to everything thrown at us, is the most significant lesson we can teach our children. If we want them to respond to failure by keeping their chin up, learning a lesson from it, and bouncing back with resilience, then we must do the same. The currency of the words we use to guide our children is only backed up by the actions of integrity with which we live our life.

According to Brené Brown, children are hard-wired for struggle. The danger comes when we try to keep our children perfect and help them avoid struggle and failure. We are all imperfect, yet we are all worthy of love and belonging, and we can all overcome adversity.[5] As leaders looking to make an impact, we must be the hero of our own journey first and live the sermon we want to preach. We don't do this by being perfect. We do this by being accountable for our mistakes and rising above them. Then, we will have gained the authority to be that mentor our children and players need to help guide them on their journey.

Mistakes, failures, and losses are going to happen so why waste our energy making excuses after they happen? Holocaust survivor Viktor Frankl said that suffering is unavoidable, but that ultimately all suffering has meaning.[6] We need to use our obstacles to find out what character we have and then show the world the greatness we have inside.

So, let our kids get out of their comfort zone, be relentless, and keep on failing! And in the locker room and on the ride home remember our kids are watching to see how we will respond as parents and coaches, so they know what it takes to be a hero.

CHAPTER 9

First Things First

What should we do when adversity strikes, or we are in a situation that we don't like? We need to respond rather than react. When we respond, we take time to think about our mission and the principles by which we want to live. Then, we summon the energy to make sure our actions align with those principles. Brené Brown defined integrity as choosing courage over comfort, practicing our values, and choosing what's right over fun, fast, and easy.[1] As parents and coaches, we should always remember to put first things first and be servant leaders.

I had recently been fired from the high school basketball coaching position that I thought I would have for the remainder of my coaching career. Our family moved to a new community, although it was somewhat familiar as my wife grew up there and it was a town that we competed against in sports each year.

I had no definitive plans for coaching. I had several people contact me about various coaching positions, but we decided to move based on what we believed was best for our family. I did not want to chase a coaching position and put our family in a situation where we would struggle, so we put first things first and did what we believed was best for our family. We put our faith in God that if I were meant to coach again, the opportunity would present itself.

Our boys had both played soccer previously, so we signed them up for the soccer league in the new community, as well as our daughter who was just now old enough to play. I was looking forward to sitting on the sidelines and telling my kids, "I love watching you play," after each game.

As the beginning of the season approached, I received an e-mail that the league needed an extra coach for the division in which one of my sons would play. I was somewhat intrigued as I still had a passion for coaching.

Soccer is a sport I have little knowledge about as I never played it as a kid and my overall experience with it was limited. I did coach my son's team of 4 and 5-year olds a few years prior to that. However, that was the age where you pretty much roll the ball out, hope that no one gets hurt, and make sure you have enough snacks and drinks for everyone. Also, I was the new guy in town so I waited and figured they would have someone else step up.

The next week a second e-mail popped up. The director said that if they could not find another coach they would have 25 players on each team. Even though this division did play the full 11 players at a time, this meant some kids would get to play less than half of each game. I knew my son would not like that and it probably would not be a great experience for all the kids.

Again, I went back and forth with myself over the pros and cons. I genuinely enjoy coaching and working with kids, but I was frustrated by all the "extracurricular activities" that go with being a head coach and are often unappreciated. After the third e-mail asking for someone to volunteer to coach, I finally relented and told the director that I would do it. We had a coaches' meeting a few days later and started practice the next week.

Using Strategy

Things started well. I enjoyed working with the kids and helping them improve. I was trying to learn more about soccer and started thinking about strategies for putting us in position to be the best we could be.

Our first game rolled around, and we won 3-1. The kids played great, and it was fun. I later found out that one of our opponent's best players was out of town and had missed the game. We lost the next game 2-1 and were set to face what I thought was the best team in the division.

It was my philosophy that every player should learn to play different positions. So in addition to making sure each player received approximately the same amount of playing time, I spent about an hour each Friday night drawing up the lineups and putting the kids in positions. I had a general idea of where each kid liked to play and I usually let them play there at least one rotation. However, I would also put them in other positions so they could be out of their comfort zone. The only position I did not make them play was goalie.

For our third game against the best team, I decided to shift to a more defensive lineup. I thought that if we stacked enough people back on defense that we could at least stop them from scoring and could maybe tie them 0-0. The result was a 7-0 loss for our team that left me frustrated. I was not frustrated by losing, but that our kids seemed to be unaggressive and not enthusiastic. My wife even commented on my body language after the game.

I started going back to the ideas that I had been learning in the last few years and had helped me grow. Anything that happens to us is in our best interest and an opportunity to learn and grow.[2] How can I use this situation to become a better person? I realized I had been focused on winning, or at least trying to tie, and I forgot to put first things first.

Playing for Innocence

Part of my frustration was continually having the players ask me if they could play a specific position. In fact, after that 7-0 defeat, I told them that they could no longer tell me they wanted to play a particular position unless I asked them. I said my objectives were for the kids to give their best effort, have a great attitude, treat other people well, and try to learn as much as they could so they could improve. But I had fallen back into the trap that if I could orchestrate our team to win, then that would prove our kids were reaching their potential.

Duke University basketball coach Mike Krzyzewski explained when he was growing up in Chicago in the 1950's there were no organized leagues with adults in charge. It was the kids organizing themselves into teams and, although they were trying to win the game, they were playing for the enjoyment and innocence of the game.[3]

I finally realized that maybe the kids were not aggressive because I was putting them in positions they did not like. Also, I had changed our strategy, and they were confused as to what I wanted. I decided that at the next practice we would practice a new strategy. When I subbed them into the game, I would only tell them who to go in for, and they could play any position they wanted to. This new plan would save me from having to spend so much time drawing up lineups, and I thought they would give a better effort if they were able to play where they wanted.

John Wooden said, "When you start thinking about winning, you stop thinking about doing your job."[4] I had overloaded the kids with so much game strategy that they had forgotten to do their job...play hard and have fun. And I had forgotten to do mine...create an environment where the kids played for a love of the game and improved no matter what the scoreboard said.

Would the Experiment Work?

Unfortunately, our practice for the week was rained out. So after our warm-ups before our next game, I gathered the kids together and asked them what position they wanted to play. I explained that they could play whatever position they wanted to. We had generally lined up with three forwards (offense), four midfielders (offense and defense), three defenders (defense), and a goalie.

I had no idea how this would work out. We could end up with ten forwards and one goalie. But I had a good feeling that they would give a better effort as they didn't have to worry about "strategy". The looks on their faces when I explained this to them gave me a good feeling.

We were playing one of the teams who I thought we probably should beat. We tied 1-1. But "we" had a great time. We had about six or seven more shots to score our second goal. We also had a ball that slipped through our goalie's hand, went through his legs, and he turned around and saved a couple of inches before crossing the line. I asked the kids after the game if they had fun and it was a loud and emphatic "YES!" That yes had nothing to do with the scoreboard. Rather, it had everything to do with them giving their best effort and enjoying the experience.

I also realized during the game I could concentrate on affirming and encouraging the kids rather than worry about making sure they were staying in the right positions. The following week when we sent the kids out on the field to start the game they were communicating and directing each other where to line up, and they had a balanced lineup. A smile crept across my face as I realized that by taking away some of my control I was teaching them to problem-solve on their own.

Who Are We Serving?

According to Jon Gordon, we can't serve ourselves and our team at the same time. And if we want to create a legacy that will help change the world we must choose to serve our team.[5] I had lost my focus by trying to prove I could coach by winning games and when a coach does that they are not serving their players. Does this mean a coach should not study the X's and O's and strategies to help the team? Not at all. That is a relevant technical aspect of the coach's job. There are many different X's and O's that can be effective in a sport, but those X's and O's by themselves won't teach the people we are coaching how to be good husbands or wives, how to be good employees or bosses, or how to be good citizens and neighbors.

On the soccer field, we achieved our objectives by putting first things first and having the right perspective. For me, it was a double win. I used this situation to become better, and I helped others do their best as well. I agree with Clint Hurdle, the manager of the Pittsburgh Pirates, who expressed he wants to win, but he is more interested in turning his players into winners.[6] The scoreboard doesn't determine whether we are a winner or not; it is how we play the game. And sometimes the kids just need the adults to get out of the way for that to happen.

In 20 years, most of us probably won't remember the scores of those games, but hopefully, we will treasure the lessons learned and put first things first.

CHAPTER 10

Identity Foreclosure

What do you want to be when you grow up?

We often receive these subtle hints that our identity should be wrapped up in what we do, the position we have, or other symbols of status. It can be dangerous to place our identity and worth into material possessions and other external factors that can be taken away at any time and, in the grand scheme of life, do not matter.

One of the co-founders of the What Drives Winning movement, Brett Ledbetter, explained that the idea of identity foreclosure is finding our identity in the external results of our competitive experience. Brett interviewed a 19-year-old girl who was one of the top players in her sport for her age. She was struggling because she no longer felt joy as a result of her participation. Every one of her performances was analyzed, and if she didn't score a goal, then the message from coaches and others was that something was wrong. Brett asked her how she would have felt when she was 13 years old if he had told her all the accomplishments she would accrue by the time she was 19. She would have claimed those accomplishments would make her the happiest girl in the world. However, she did accomplish all those things and she was unhappy.[1] The expectations placed on young people to perform can often make them find their value through that performance. They often feel loved when they perform well and feel abandoned when they do not. Although the term identity foreclosure may not be familiar to all of us, it is an idea so simple that a 4-year old can understand it.

Just Have Fun

We signed our daughter, Hannah, up to play soccer when she was four years old. We are a sports family, and often when her brothers are shooting baskets, Hannah wants me to pick her up and let her shoot the ball in the basket. She loves to bump the volleyball back and forth with my wife or me. And she will often get out and kick the soccer ball around with her brothers.

When soccer practice started, she was a little nervous, and we weren't surprised as she had not even started preschool yet. She was great at kicking the ball when they lined up in front of the goal, but as soon as there were offense and defense, she did not want to get in and kick the ball.

If you have ever witnessed soccer at this age, you know it is essentially a herd of kids chasing the ball up and down the field. As the games started, we found out that Hannah's mode of operation was to be just outside the herd, but always from behind and at a safe distance.

Occasionally, on the way to practice or games, Hannah would say that she didn't want to go or that she didn't want to kick the ball. We would respond, "That's okay. All you have to do is have fun." And once we got there, she did! She would be all smiles as she stayed behind the herd.

Toward the end of the season, as we were riding home from practice, I told Hannah that if she wanted to try something else like gymnastics or another activity we could do that instead of soccer.

Hannah said that she did not want to.

Our son Jacob said, "Well if you don't play sports, then what are you going to be when you grow up?"

She responded, "I just want to be Hannah."

For some people that may have broken their heart, but I couldn't have been prouder.

A Support System

Hannah understands who we are as a person is more important than what we do as a player. Identity foreclosure happens when we lose that perspective and put the emphasis on what we do as a player and the results we get (or don't get) over who we are as a person.

Joe Ehrmann declared the most competitive sport in America is parenting.[2] In some cases, we are living vicariously through our children and hope that their performance will give us a sense of approval or superiority. Sometimes we try to cover it up by saying that we are just trying to teach our kids to be more competitive. We should treat the opportunity to play sports as an honor, and it should be enjoyed regardless of the score, according to Ehrmann. And when we are having fun and enjoying the camaraderie of our teammates, team performance improves as a by-product.[3] But we need an environment that supports having fun and enjoying the opportunity to play sports.

Mike Krzyzewski explained that as a child his parents supported everything he did. His confidence as an adult stemmed from the fact that he was not afraid to lose due to the love and pride he felt in his home environment.[4] If we watch Krzyzewski coach on the sidelines at Duke University, we can see he is pretty competitive. After growing up in Chicago, he attended the U.S. Military Academy at West Point and participated in basketball for four years before becoming a coach and going on to win five NCAA National

Championships. But for him, it all started with that loving support system he had growing up that emphasized doing what you love, doing it to the best of your ability, and letting the results take care of themselves.

According to Carol Dweck, this is another example of the growth mindset. Those of us with the fixed mindset focus on the outcome and think if the outcome is bad, then everything in the process was a waste. Conversely, those of us with the growth mindset value what we are doing regardless of the result.[5] Many of us with the growth mindset do end up achieving things as a by-product of our enthusiasm, but even if we do not reach the desired outcome, we can still find value in the journey to get there.

Life is Too Short to Grind

But don't we have to be serious and competitive and grind through things we don't like to do to be the best in the game? The "grind" is a term that has become popular to show we are putting in the necessary work so we can achieve something.

The "grind" is simply something we tolerate, not something from which we learn. If we hate the process then we are only doing it for the results, and the results are not always under our control, so we are allowing our sport, job, or activity to use us.

What happens at the end of the "grind" if we don't get the results we want? Only 50% of the people involved win each game. What if two competitors have grinded an equal amount in practice and equally in the game? Someone is still going to lose.

If we are doing it for the enjoyment, then we will be more motivated to stick with it. If we are learning, then we will have a better chance to improve and win the next time around. If we are always alert, then we will be ready to pivot in life and seize opportunities that present themselves rather than having tunnel vision and keep grinding into a situation that is limiting us from realizing our full potential.

Life is too short to grind. We should enjoy what we do or find something else. Many of us lament we do not have a vocation that we sincerely enjoy and are passionate about. We should be doing everything we can to find what sets our soul on fire. The same logic applies to our kids playing sports. We should be helping them discover what they are genuinely passionate about and let that passion bring out their competitiveness. But if we try to force the competitiveness into them it will lead to a situation like the 19-year-old girl interviewed by Brett Ledbetter. She may be one of the top players in her arena, but the joy of playing the sport was stripped away by identity foreclosure.

If we are in a situation we feel we cannot get out of then we need to use our experience to learn everything we can and mold ourselves into the person we want to be. Everything that happens to us is an opportunity for us to learn and grow. Quit grinding and start learning! Quit grinding and start enjoying! Quit grinding and start living!

Hannah is tall for her age; she does a great job bumping the volleyball, is pretty fast, and can kick a soccer ball really hard. But none of that matters if it is not something she truly wants to do and has a passion for. Hannah is also a sweet, sweet girl with a contagious laugh who loves her brothers and her mom and dad.

Maybe Hannah will end up being an Olympic athlete...or maybe she won't. It doesn't matter to me as long as she is still Hannah.

CHAPTER 11

The 20 Year Return

He refused to shake my hand...

We were at our end-of-season banquet, and I knew the following week I was more than likely going to be fired as the basketball coach from the same high school that I attended in the community in which I had lived 24 of the 35 years of my life. I was making sure to shake each player's hand as they were leaving. As one of the seniors walked toward me, I put out my hand. Connor had a smile on his face, but he shook his head at my hand. Instead, he put his arms out to hug me.

One of the quickest ways to lose motivation is to feel that our effort is not having an impact. It is nice to get positive feedback and hear from others we are doing a good job, but we need to have the perspective that our return on investment may not happen until 20 years down the road. Our competitive experiences through sports are an excellent opportunity to plant seeds in young people. The seeds may not produce a harvest right away, but when they do it can be a harvest of deep and lasting impact.

Seeds of Character

Connor had been a captain of our team even though he did not play that much his senior year. He had not attended many of our summer basketball activities during the previous two summers because he was working or had other commitments. Basketball was not his top priority during the off-season, and that's okay. So why was he named a captain? During the season Connor was all in. He was committed, he had a great attitude, and he was one of the best teammates you would ever want to play alongside. In short, he had the character that we wanted our basketball program to represent, and he was a great role model.

In an essay for an award he was nominated for, Connor talked about how basketball was actually his third-favorite sport, but it was the one he learned the most from in high school. He credited the character-building activities that we did as part of our program with teaching him poise and confidence to make good decisions and work with people.

In *Legacy*, James Kerr detailed the secret formula of the All Blacks, the rugby team from New Zealand which claims an 86% winning percentage as a professional sports organization. It is the foundation of the All Blacks culture that has led to their unprecedented success, and they built that foundation on character. More than physical abilities, the leaders of the All Blacks select their team members based on character. Like the teams formed by Vince Lombardi, John Wooden, and Bill Walsh, the key is to create a culture with a high standard of integrity and doing things the right way, and the results will take care of themselves.[1]

The basis of character for the All Blacks is humility, which they reveal by their ritual of sweeping the sheds. After the game, the team leaders clean up their dressing and training area themselves with brooms. This illustrates their humility and the fact that everything must be earned rather than handed to them.[2] By creating an environment that supports personal development, a group can reap the rewards of increased performance as a benefit. We reveal our character in our actions, which are a result of our principles and values. The question is what do we value...an impact that will fade away or one that will remain forever?

Coaching the Long Game

The idea of the 20-year return originated with Amos Alonzo Stagg, the legendary football coach at the University of Chicago in the early 20th century. After winning a championship, a reporter asked Coach Stagg what he thought about his team. Coach Stagg said he wouldn't really know about his team for another 20 years. He knew that his most noble role was developing people, not winning championships, and sometimes those people would not take advantage of the lessons he was teaching until much later.

Mike Krzyzewski actually thinks that having a goal to win the national championship or win a certain number of games is a shallow goal. As a coach, he feels if the only reason he is in his profession is to win games then he is going to have a pretty hollow existence.[3] There is a difference between happiness and fulfillment. Happiness usually deals with our feelings in the present and our current circumstances. Fulfillment has more endurance and can last even in tough times. It is okay to want to be happy, but it is impossible for us to be happy all the time.

For example, when we lose a loved one we are not going to be happy. We are going to feel sadness, grief, and possibly many other emotions. At the same time, we can still experience fulfillment from the relationship we had with the person and be grateful for the opportunity to experience life with them while they were with us. The same can be true of our competitive experience. We may not always be happy with the outcome, but we can always experience fulfillment if we gave our best effort. We can appreciate the opportunity to play, the relationships we developed, and the lessons we learned through our experience.

A Harvest of Impact

As parents and coaches, we often want to fix our children and players, but we need to take the approach of a farmer. Rather than trying to force our will on people, we should be like farmers who are always planting seeds.[4] We often want to see the seeds sprout and bloom right away but that does not always happen. The seeds we plant are the words, ideas, principles, and values we teach our children and players. The sunlight and water are the examples we produce as role models by the lives we live. We can plant the seeds by talking the talk, but we must provide the sunlight and water by walking the walk; otherwise, the seeds will not grow.

You may have heard the story of the Chinese bamboo tree that does not show any signs of growth in the first five years of its life. However, if appropriately watered, it will grow 90 feet in six weeks in the fifth year. Sometimes there does not appear to be any growth, but we have planted the seeds, and the roots are growing strong to build a foundation that can support massive growth.

When we are planting seeds, we have to realize leaders of impact take time to develop and grow. According to John Maxwell's Law of Exponential Growth, if we want to grow our organization we should lead followers, but if we are going to multiply the impact of our group we need to lead leaders.[5] These leaders need life experiences to help mold and shape them. So we cannot get caught up wondering why we are not getting more positive results sooner. When we lead with integrity and lead by principles, we must trust that the long-term effects have a far more significant impact than the quick fixes that we all want to make us feel good.

I did not make Connor great. Connor just revealed the greatness that he had within him. And we all have our unique greatness within us. Hopefully, we created an environment with our basketball program that helped Connor see greatness within himself. Some players have the perspective to reveal their greatness sooner than others. Maybe it will take one year or perhaps it will take 20 years. Jon Gordon said most of the time people will not recognize or appreciate us for our work, and that's okay. Just keep doing the work. Keep making a difference. We'll be glad we did.[6] We have to rise above the need for instant gratification and lead with the perspective of the 20-year return.

CHAPTER 12

Do You Have Any Suggestions for Improvement?

In an interview with the What Drives Winning organization, Dr. Carol Dweck challenged parents to ask their children two questions about their sports experience:

1. Do you feel judged on the car ride home?

2. Do you feel pressure to have a certain outcome of a game in order to make me proud?[1]

These are questions that might be uncomfortable for some of us, but they cut right to the heart of the relationship we have with our children concerning their competitive experience. If we can create an environment free of judgment and pressure, then we can flip the script to allow our children to take control of their learning and growth.

Asking questions is one of the best ways for us to learn and grow. When we are young, we are pretty good at asking questions as we discover the world. Possibly the most significant question we can ask is, "Why?" Understanding the reason behind an idea or principle is powerful. We need to encourage those we lead to ask questions, probe, and be curious. If we ignite the fire of curiosity, it will not only give young people autonomy, but it will hopefully inspire them to chase mastery as well.

Who is Asking the Question?

One summer our son participated in a basketball shootout where he played three games in one day. He played well, but there were a few things I noticed he needed to focus on for improvement. However, I decided that I could address them later that night or even the next day. It was not anything I was upset about, but just some suggestions for improvement. Unfortunately, I would not get the chance to bring it up with my son.

After the last game, Nathan was walking towards me and wanted to know where we were going to eat because he wanted to invite one of his friends from the team. I told him that I had already planned to let him pick where to eat. So Nathan picked the spot and invited his friend. As we were walking out of the gym, I told Nathan that I loved watching him play and that I thought he was making some big improvements.

Then in the car on the way to the restaurant, Nathan asked, "Do you have any suggestions for improvement?"

Wow!

Verbally, I gave Nathan the few simple suggestions that I had wanted to tell him to help him improve, but internally I was like Rocky Balboa at the top of the steps to the Philadelphia Museum of Art!

According to Dr. Dweck's work, this is a sign of a growth mindset. People with a fixed mindset believe their talent level or intelligence is set at birth, so they are continually trying to prove themselves; people with a growth mindset understand they are competing against their best self and are invariably looking for ways to improve.[2]

When we praise a child's talent or abilities, we are promoting a fixed mindset. The response to this is not to improve, but to compare ourselves to others so that we can prove our superiority. If we need to put other people down to prove our superiority, then so be it. If we need to blame the referees or the coach to prove our superiority, then so be it.

But when we praise their effort and love watching them play, we take away all the pressure they have to try to prove themselves. They have nothing to prove because they know they have our love either way. They will see that effort leads to improvement and everyone loves to get better.

Mastery

According to Self-Determination Theory, the three most prominent sources of internal motivation are autonomy, mastery, and relatedness. Autonomy means having the control to decide what to do with our lives. Mastery means wanting to be good at something for its own sake. Relatedness means being connected to other human beings and working to make a difference in the world.[3]

It is crucial to note mastery does not have anything to do with comparing ourselves to others. Mastery does not mean mastery over the competition. Instead, it signifies mastery of our capabilities and realizing our best self. We can defeat an opponent but not come anywhere close to fulfilling our capabilities. Likewise, we can lose on the scoreboard while reaching our full potential at that given moment. Mastery is indeed a standard of excellence. We must relentlessly pursue how we can become the best we are capable of becoming.

Olympian Adam Kreek acknowledged the obvious goal of an athletic contest is to win, but too much focus on the result hinders performance. Rather, the ultimate goal is to discover and reveal our "authentic, best self."[4] This journey means removing the self-imposed timeline of when we think we, or our children, need to "make it". There is no finish line for excellence because we do not know the actual limits of our capabilities. The right environment is one that allows participants to fall in love with the process of striving for that vision of their best self and victory will often come along as a by-product. In order to attain mastery, we need to be given the autonomy to internalize the quest for excellence.

Feedback is essential for growth, but some of the best feedback we can ever receive is from ourselves in the form of self-evaluation. It is vital that we reflect on our experiences and learn from them. Once we are comfortable evaluating ourselves, it becomes much easier to ask someone else to add feedback to our evaluation cycle. Former NFL head coach Herm Edwards concluded it is crucial to tell people the "why" behind what they are doing.[5] Merely telling someone to do something does not give them autonomy. Explaining the "why" provides the person with the independence to conscientiously decide if they believe they agree with what they are doing. Without the "why" they can always respond they are only doing what someone told them to do. With the knowledge of the "why" each person can now decide whether the action falls in line with their principles and values.

One of the lessons I learned from this situation is patience. I could have yelled my suggestions to Nathan during the game. I could have immediately given him my ideas after the game. But by being patient, I found out that Nathan has started to internalize his level of effort and his improvement.

I have also learned if you create the right environment people will display greatness on their own. As my wife and I have started telling our kids we love watching them play over the last couple years, sometimes we get no reaction from them. But no reaction does not mean there is not an impact.

A Better Life

It has probably been said for thousands of years, "We want our kids to have a better life than we did." In fact, many parents might say they want to GIVE their kids a better life. As incredible as this sounds, it can be crippling to our children. It should be our mission to help our children RISE ABOVE and build the character to enjoy life no matter what storms they face.

First, we all appreciate things that we work hard for and earn much more than something that we receive without any effort. Whether it is a job, an award, or money, we value things that we had to toil and struggle to obtain. This awareness is not so much about the external prize, but it is the feelings we experience by digging down deep to develop our character, and that is something no one can take away from us.

The same is true in relationships. Conflict is going to happen but the relationships that we put the time and effort into usually bring the most satisfaction. So we need to understand that having to strive for a good life is actually a pretty amazing thing.

Second, we need to be clear on what we mean by a better life. Do we mean a lot of money? Do we mean happiness? Do we mean not having to work? Do we mean gaining fulfillment through serving others? Do we mean growing to be the best we can be and having an impact on the world? Everything we do for ourselves will fade away when we are gone, but everything we do for others will remain behind.

If we look at any great figure like Abraham Lincoln, Mother Teresa, or Martin Luther King, Jr., I doubt we will be talking about how much money they had, the clothes that they wore, or the type of car (or buggy) they drove. Their legacy is the impact they had on others. And they all had struggles!

We would be crazy to say those great people had a comfortable life. In fact, it is their struggles with the human experience and their ability to overcome them that we love so much about them. So why do we want our children to have a relaxing and care-free life? That is most definitely the way to assure they will not have a positive impact on the world.

So are we saying we should intentionally make our kids' lives miserable? Not at all. The world is full of enough heartache and suffering that we do not have to go looking for it. But rather than spending our energy trying to help our children avoid struggles and adversity, we should be acting as guides and mentors. We should be supporting them to maneuver through stressful situations and show them how they can use their experiences to build character so they can change the world.

So the next time our child is upset about a tough situation, we need to take a deep breath and switch from rescue mode to mentor mode. We can rise above the need to protect our child from adversity and teach them how they can use their obstacles to push themselves to greater heights. Not only will they improve their own lives, but they will inspire countless others around them to do the same.

Enjoy the Ride

When we start telling our kids we love watching them play, it will often feel awkward in the beginning. But we should have a growth mindset about being a parent who is helping our child with their competitive experience. When we are traveling on the success road, we often get off course and need some gentle guidance to get back on track.

Remember fear, incentive, and love represent our primary motivators. Paulo Coelho observed, "When you are loved, you can do anything in creating. When you are loved, there's no need at all to understand what is happening, because everything happens within you."[6] Love will not only endure longer, but it will make the ride a whole lot more enjoyable!

Epilogue:
Live Our Legacy

So how do we take this information and use it on a daily basis? Every day we have a choice in many different situations, and those decisions are creating our legacy. Here are some things to keep in mind as we are living our legacy.

#1 Forget About Titles

First, and foremost, we have to lead ourselves and leadership is not about positions, titles, money, degrees, or power. Leadership is possible for every person in every situation. In fact, if leadership is influence then we are automatically a leader because there is always someone watching us for guidance or learning from our example. So make sure we are leading them in a positive direction.

#2 Know Our Why

One of the questions children always ask is, "Why?" The ultimate "why" question is why are we here? We must have an awareness of our purpose and mission in life. Our purpose is our foundation and our guide, but it must be deeper than ourselves. We will not impact the world by simply chasing our own selfish desires. Know our why and we will truly know ourselves.

#3 Esse Quam Videri

Esse Quam Videri (Latin for "to be, rather than to seem") is the truth of who we are at the present moment. This understanding is a combination of the actions we take and the motivation and beliefs behind those actions. People make mistakes, and people can change but, ultimately, our actions reveal our principles and our values.

#4 Train for Excellence

We all have a unique greatness within us, but the quickest way to prevent that greatness from being revealed is to compare ourselves to others. We must focus on running our own race and seeking excellence in all we do. By pushing ourselves to bring out our best in each situation our best shot will keep getting better and better each time. When we train for excellence, we can stay humble in victory and focused in defeat.

#5 Don't Do It For the Applause

Life is a journey, but it should not be a chase. There is no finish line or destination to reach because we have everything we need for our journey inside of us. Life is about finding the greatness we have inside and then giving it away to the rest of the world through the relationships and connections we create.

Former college basketball coach and television commentator Jim Valvano died from cancer in 1993. During his final months, he spent many hours sharing and connecting with friend and fellow coach Mike Krzyzewski. Coach K commented there are two things Jim said during that time that had a tremendous impact on him. First, Valvano said he did not do it right by spending so much time trying to achieve things, rather than take care of himself and spend more time with his family. The second impactful statement he made was, "A person really doesn't become whole until he becomes a part of something that's bigger than himself."[1]

If we have a desire to impact this world, then we must understand we create an impact through an inside-out process. We must first look inside ourselves to determine what we can contribute to the world and how we can grow our character. But in order to reach our true potential, we must use our gifts to improve the lives of others. Viktor Frankl called this the "self-transcendence of human existence."[2] It is only through the process of giving away our gifts that we are completely able to reach our true individual potential.

As parents and coaches, we need to have the perspective of using our gifts to improve the lives of our children by helping them build character and learn life lessons through their competitive experiences.

I believe deep down we all know what the most important things in life are and we truly want to live a life of joy and meaning. I hope this book helps inspire us to evaluate our perspective, put first things first, and rise above our storms so we can enjoy the journey as we soar to new heights and live our legacy!

Want to Take
the Next Step?

7 Day Journal Writing Challenge

Go to www.riseaboveleadership.com/7-day-journal-writing-challenge and enter your e-mail address to receive prompts to help you give your BEST SHOT to improve 1% each day!

Want to Connect?

Website: www.riseaboveleadership.com

Twitter: @jonbarth11

Facebook: www.facebook.com/riseaboveleadership/

Instagram: jon.barth.11

E-mail: jon@riseaboveleadership.com

Suggested Reading List

Reading has been the foundation for my own personal transformation so I would like to share some of the books that have had the greatest impact on me!

To view a full list of our reading recommendations visit www.riseaboveleadership.com/library

The Bible
No Greater Love by Mother Teresa
The Strange Secret of the Big Time by Frosty Westering
The Only Way to Win by Jim Loehr
InSideOut Coaching by Joe Erhmann
What Drives Winning by Brett Ledbetter
The Leader Who Had No Title by Robin Sharma
Burn Your Goals by Joshua Medcalf and Jamie Gilbert
Chop Wood Carry Water by Joshua Medcalf
The Principle Circle by Jamie Gilbert
The Obstacle is the Way by Ryan Holiday
Mindset by Carol Dweck
The Art of Work by Jeff Goins
Mentally Tough Teens by Justin Su'a
Take the Stairs by Rory Vaden
Leaders Eat Last by Simon Sinek
The Contrarian's Guide to Leadership by Steven Sample

You Win in the Locker Room First by Jon Gordon and Mike Smith

The Carpenter by Jon Gordon

Training Camp by Jon Gordon

The Hard Hat by Jon Gordon

Toughness by Jay Bilas

A Coach and a Miracle by Jim Johnson and Mike Latona

Wooden on Leadership by John Wooden and Steve Jamison

The Champion's Mind by Jim Afremow

Boundaries by Henry Cloud and John Townsend

Legacy by James Kerr

In a Pit With a Lion on a Snowy Day by Mark Batterson

Leading With the Heart by Mike Krzyzewski

The Score Takes Care of Itself by Bill Walsh

The Matheny Manifesto by Mike Matheny

Shaken by Tim Tebow

Wooden by Seth Davis

Eleven Rings by Phil Jackson

The Traveler's Gift by Andy Andrews

The Alchemist by Paulo Coelho

Profiles in Courage by John F. Kennedy

Braving the Wilderness by Brené Brown

The Four Agreements by Don Miguel Ruiz

The 21 Irrefutable Laws of Leadership by John Maxwell

About the Author

Jon believes it is possible for everyone to attain success because success is the process of striving to achieve excellence, which is living up to our full potential. This journey involves giving it our best shot each day in order to improve in body, mind, and soul.

Jon founded Rise Above Leadership with the mission to inspire leaders to rise above and enjoy the journey as they live their legacy! Through his experience, he has found our perspectives can catapult us toward excellence or hold us back from reaching our potential. He loves learning from others but has found we often gain the most wisdom by reflecting on our own experiences and extracting the valuable lessons from our everyday lives.

Jon has coaching experience at the junior high, high school, and college levels and has worked as a teacher and administrator in public education. He has earned a Master's degree in Education Administration from William Woods University as well as a Master's degree in Coaching from Greenville College. However, his most important mission is to follow God and lead his family, his wife Sarah, and their children Nathan, Jacob, and Hannah who bring a tremendous amount of joy to his life.

Notes

INTRODUCTION

[1] Wooden, John (with Steve Jamison). *Wooden on Leadership: How to Create a Winning Organization*. McGraw-Hill, 2005, p. 80.

PLAY FOR THE LOVE OF THE GAME

[1] Brown, Les. *Live Your Dreams*. HarperCollins, 1992, p. 70.

[2] Pizza, Angelo and De Haven, Carter (Producers) & Anspaugh, David (Director). *Hoosiers*. Orion, 1986.

[3] King, Jay. "Boston Celtics news 2013: Brad Stevens discusses how he'll handle losses, why he's so reserved after big wins." http://www.masslive.com/celtics/in-dex.ssf/2013/09/how_does_brad_stevens_handle_l.html (accessed October 6, 2017).

[4] Wooden, *Wooden on Leadership*, p. 107-114.

WOULD YOU RATHER...?

[1] Westering, Frosty. *The Strange Secret of the Big Time*. Big Five Productions, 2005, 70-71.

[2] Ibid, 71-72.

[3] Ibid, 75-76.

[4] Gordon, Jon. *The Energy Bus: 10 Rules to Fuel Your Life, Work, and Team with Positive Energy*. Wiley, 2007, p. 131.

[5] Maxwell, John. *The 21 Irrefutable Laws of Leadership: Follow Them and People Will Follow You*. Thomas Nelson, 2007, pp. 23-25.

[6] Medcalf, Joshua & Jamie Gilbert. *Burn Your Goals: The Counter Cultural Approach to Achieving Your Greatest Potential*. Lulu, 2014, p. 38.

[7] Johnson, Jim (with Mike Latona). *A Coach and a Miracle: Life Lessons from a Man Who Believed in an Autistic Boy*. HeartBridge Press, 2017.

[8] Wooden, *Wooden on Leadership*, pp. 38-40.

REVEAL OUR GREATNESS

[1] Wooden, *Wooden on Leadership*, p. 20.

BE POSITIVE

[1] Krzyzewski, Mike (with Donald Phillips). *Leading With the Heart: Coach K's Successful Strategies for Basketball, Business, and Life*. Grand Central, 2000, p. 153.

[2] Ruiz, Don Miguel (with Janet Mills). *The Four Agreements: A Toltec Wisdom Book*. Amber-Allen, 1997, p. 26.

[3] Kouzes, Jim and Posner, Barry. *The Leadership Challenge: How to Make Extraordinary Things Happen in Organizations*. Wiley, 2017.

LET THE SCORE TAKE CARE OF ITSELF

[1] Jackson, Phil (and Hugh Delehanty). *Eleven Rings: The Soul of Success*. Penguin, 2013, p. 23.

[2] Walsh, Bill (with Steve Jamison and Craig Walsh). *The Score Takes Care of Itself: My Philosophy of Leadership*. Penguin, 2009.

[3] Ledbetter, Brett (Producer). (September 13, 2015). *The Truth About Achievement*. Retrieved from
https://www.youtube.com/watch?v=81eRabHiZx0

[4] Loehr, Jim. *The Only Way to Win: How Building Character Drives Higher Achievement and Greater Fulfillment in Business and Life*. Hyperion, 2012, pp. 71-80.

[5] Ibid.

[6] Jackson, *Eleven Rings*, p. 24.

[7] Ibid, 334.

I LOVE WATCHING YOU PLAY

[1] TEDx Talks (Producer). (June 20, 2014). *Changing the game in youth sports*. Retrieved from
https://www.youtube.com/watch?v=VXw0XGOVQvw&t=729s

[2] Dweck, Carol. *Mindset: The New Psychology of Success*. Random House, 2016, p. 45.

3 Dictionary.com. Retrieved from http://www.diction-ary.com/browse/success?s=t

4 Dictionary.com. Retrieved from http://www.diction-ary.com/browse/achievement?s=t

5 Wooden, *Wooden on Leadership*, p. 3.

6 Westering, *The Strange Secret of the Big Time*.

THE COACH IS THE STUDENT

1 Bilas, Jay. *Toughness: Developing True Strength On and Off the Court*. New American Library, 2013, p. 151.

2 Disabato, Pat. (March 30, 2017). Stagg boys basketball coach John Daniels cites family, resigns after 14 seasons. Chicago Tribune: Daily Southtown. Retrieved from http://www.chicagotribune.com/suburbs/daily-southtown/sports/ct-sta-boys-basketball-stagg-john-daniels-st-0331-20170330-story.html

3 Ehrmann, Joe (with Paula Ehrmann and Gregory Jordan). *In-SideOut Coaching: How Sports Can Transform Lives*. Simon & Schuster, 2011, p. 5.

4 Loehr, *The Only Way to Win*, p. 9

5 Wenzlaff, Rachel. (March 29, 2015). Eddie Reese. The Daily Texan. Retrieved from https://www.dailytexanonline.com/person/eddie-reese

6 Wooden, *Wooden on Leadership*, p. 204.

[7] Mochari, Ilan. (March 13, 2015). 7 Leadership Lessons from John Wooden's Final Title. Retrieved from https://www.inc.com/ilan-mochari/john-wooden-ucla.html

[8] Krzyzewski, *Leading with the Heart*, p. 113.

[9] Ibid, p. 114.

[10] AZ Quotes. Retrieved from http://www.azquotes.com/author/23236-Eddie_Reese

[11] TED (Producer). (January 3, 2011). *The Power of Vulnerability*. Retrieved from https://www.youtube.com/watch?v=iCvms-MzIF7o

KEEP ON FAILING

[1] Holiday, Ryan. *The Obstacle is the Way: The Timeless Art of Turning Trials into Triumph*. Penguin Group, 2014, p. 3.

[2] Dweck, *Mindset*, pp. 23-24.

[3] Krzyzewski, *Leading With the Heart*, p. 111.

[4] Tull, Thomas (Producer) & Helgeland, Brian (Director). *42*. Legendary, 2013.

[5] TED, *The Power of Vulnerability*, https://www.youtube.com/watch?v=iCvmsMzIF7o

[6] Frankl, Viktor. *Man's Search for Meaning*. Beacon Press, 2006, p. 67.

FIRST THINGS FIRST

[1] TED, *The Power of Vulnerability*,
https://www.youtube.com/watch?v=iCvmsMzIF7o

[2] Medcalf and Gilbert, *Burn Your Goals*, p. 81.

[3] Krzyzewski, *Leading With the Heart*, p. 22.

[4] Wooden, *Wooden on Leadership*, p. 216.

[5] Gordon, Jon & Mike Smith. *You Win in the Locker Room First: The 7 C's to Build a Winning Team in Sports, Business, and Life*. Wiley, 2015, pp. 88-90.

[6] Ibid, pp. 107-08.

IDENTITY FORECLOSURE

[1] Ledbetter, *The Truth About Achievement*,
https://www.youtube.com/watch?v=81eRabHiZx0

[2] Ehrmann, *InSideOut Coaching*, p. 51.

[3] Ibid, p. 90.

[4] Krzyzewski, *Leading with the Heart*, p. 12.

[5] Dweck, *Mindset*, p. 45.

THE 20 YEAR RETURN

[1] Kerr, James. *Legacy: What the All Blacks Can Teach Us About the Business of Life*. Constable, 2013, pp. 7-18.

[2] Ibid.

[3] Krzyzewski, *Leading With the Heart*, pp. 54, 60.

[4] Ledbetter, Brett (Producer). (November 8, 2015). *Billy Donovan: A Coach's Legacy*. Retrieved from https://www.youtube.com/watch?v=_YRN1K7BlpY

[5] Maxwell, *The 21 Irrefutable Laws of Leadership*, p. 245.

[6] Gordon, Jon. (April 10, 2017). Ignore the Critics: Do the Work. Retrieved from http://www.jongordon.com/positivetip/critics.html

DO YOU HAVE ANY SUGGESTIONS FOR IMPROVEMENT?

[1] What Drives Winning. (June 9, 2017). Retrieved from https://twitter.com/WDWconvo/status/873195560617918464

[2] Dweck, *Mindset*, pp.6-7.

[3] Loehr, *The Only Way to Win*, pp. 64-67

[4] Afremow, Jim. *The Champion's Mind: How Great Athletes Think, Train, and Thrive*. Rodale, 2013, pp. 190-193.

[5] Bilas, *Toughness*, p. 227.

[6] Coelho, Paulo. *The Alchemist*. HarperCollins, 1994, p. 152.

EPILOGUE: LIVE OUR LEGACY

[1] Krzyzewski, *Leading With the Heart*, p. 254.

[2] Frankl, *Man's Search for Meaning*, p. 110.

www.ingramcontent.com/pod-product-compliance
Lightning Source LLC
Chambersburg PA
CBHW070810050426
42452CB00011B/1983